Nothing is Empty:
A Whole Haiku World

Also by Robert Epstein:

A Walk around Spring Lake: Haiku

(Editor) *Beyond the Grave: Contemporary Afterlife Haiku*

(Editor) *The Breath of Surrender: A Collection of Recovery-Oriented Haiku*

Checkout Time is Noon: Death Awareness Haiku

Checkout Time is Soon: More Death Awareness Haiku

(Editor) *Dreams Wander On: Contemporary Poems of Death Awareness*

(Co-Editor with Miriam Wald) *Every Chicken, Cow, Fish and Frog: Animal Rights Haiku*

Haiku Days of Remembrance: In Honor of My Father

Free to Dance Forever: Mourning Haiku for My Mother

Haiku Edge: New & Selected Poems

Haiku Forest Afterlife

Healing into Haiku: On Illness and Pain

(Editor) *Now This: Contemporary Poems of Beginnings, Renewals, and Firsts*

(With Stacy Taylor) *Suffering Buddha: The Zen Way Beyond Health and Illness*

(Compiler with Sherry Phillips) *The Natural Man: Selected Quotations of Henry D. Thoreau*

(Editor) *The Sacred in Contemporary Haiku*

(Editor) *The Temple Bell Stops: Contemporary Poems of Grief, Loss and Change*

(Editor) *They Gave Us Life: Mothers, Fathers & Others in Haiku*

Turkey Heaven: Animal Rights Haiku

Nothing is Empty:
A Whole Haiku World

by
Robert Epstein

2019

Nothing is Empty: A Whole Haiku World
Copyright © 2019 Robert Epstein
All rights reserved.

ISBN 978-1-7325023-7-6

Cover art, "Mountains Go on Walking," by Ron C. Moss.
Used by Permission.

www.ronmoss.com

Empty Boat image in the public domain;
accessed at www.pexels.com

Middle Island Press
PO Box 354
West Union, WV 26456

The artist's job is not to succumb to despair but to find an antidote for the emptiness of existence.

~ *Woody Allen*

Form is emptiness; emptiness is form.

~ *Avalokitesvara Bodhisattva*

Nothing is permanent in this wicked world - not even our troubles.

~ *Charlie Chaplin*

Nothing in life is to be feared, it is only to be understood.

~ *Marie Curie*

Saying nothing . . . sometimes says the most.

~ *Emily Dickinson*

To be full of things is to be empty of God; to be empty of things is to be full of God.

~ *Meister Eckhart*

There is nothing permanent except change.

~ *Heraclitus*

Prayer begins at the edge of emptiness.

~ *Abraham Joshua Heschel*

Freedom is just another word/for nothing left to lose.

~ *Janis Joplin*

Look at your little finger, the emptiness of it is no different than the emptiness of infinity.

~ *Jack Kerouac*

You and nothingness are one; you and nothingness are a joint phenomenon, not two separate processes.

~ *J. Krishnamurti*

Nothing is born, nothing dies.

~ Antoine-Laurent Lavoisier

Faith includes noticing the mess, the emptiness and discomfort, and letting it be there until some light returns.

~ Anne Lamott

Grief. . . gives life a permanently provisional feeling. . . Up till this I always had too little time. Now there is nothing but time.

~ C.S. Lewis

I felt very still and empty, the way the eye of a tornado must feel, moving dully along in the middle of the surrounding hullabaloo.

~ Sylvia Plath

I am the wisest man alive, for I know one thing, and that is that I know nothing.

~ Plato

What a relief to be empty! Then God can live your life.

~ Rumi

In all our searching, the only thing that we've found that makes the emptiness bearable is each other.

~ Carl Sagan

Nothingness lies coiled in the heart of being - like a worm.

~ Jean-Paul Sartre

Never say there is nothing beautiful in the world anymore.

~ Albert Schweitzer

We say true existence comes from emptiness and goes back again into emptiness. What appears from emptiness is true existence. We have to go through the gate of emptiness.

~ Shunryu Suzuki

If you face God in prayer and silence, God will speak to you. Then you will know that you are nothing. It is only when you realize your nothingness, that God can fill you with Himself.

~ Mother Teresa

We can know only that we know nothing. And that is the highest degree of human wisdom.

~ Leo Tolstoy

I love to talk about nothing. It's the only thing I know anything about.

~ Oscar Wilde

In Loving Memory:

Pepi, Joseph, & Zoltan Deutsch

Contents

Acknowledgments — xiii

Preface — xv

Poems

    Nothing is Nothing — 1

    Nothing is Something — 21

    Nothing is Personal — 45

    Nothing is Impersonal — 65

    Emptiness is All — 89

Recommended Reading — 109

Acknowledgments

I am grateful for the ongoing support of friends and family: Janet Amptman, Clara Knopfler, Joy McCall, David H. Rosen, Jay Schlesinger, Wendy Etsuku Siu, Sophie Soltani, Stacy Taylor, Miriam Wald.

Ron C. Moss deserves my eternal gratitude for his boundless generosity and infinite talent. Ron's art reflects his big, wide, extraordinary heart and mind.

Once again, I wish to thank Christina Taylor, publisher at Middle Island Press, for her enthusiastic and outstanding help in publishing this book.

Preface

If knowledge of mysteries comes after emptiness of mind, that is illumination of heart.

~ *Rumi*

Much Ado about Something

In the West, we are urged from an early age to *make something* of ourselves. (My mother expected me to become the first Jewish President of the United States!) We strive, aspire, compete in hopes of excelling and gaining recognition for our outstanding achievements. A lot may be sacrificed along the way, including our hearts and minds, friendships and Nature. Yet, in the end, we die, we become nothing — the apparent antithesis of all we have ventured to accomplish. Does death render this lifetime of striving null and void? Is nothingness or emptiness part of a cruel joke that Life plays on us, making a mockery of our ego-driven ambitions?

With a Little Help: Taoism and Zen

I have long-wondered whether nothing or emptiness might nudge us to *wake up* from the trance of striving or becoming, if we would but give nothing our full attention. It is a subject well-worth contemplating, and that is what I endeavor to do in these pages. *Nothing appears everywhere*, and that seems to be no coincidence. According to Ray Grigg in *The Tao of Zen*:

> Emptiness is a special kind of something. The walls of houses divide it rooms. Bottles would be useless without it. The limits of all things are defined by it. Everything that exists is contained in emptiness. Emptiness is what everything else cannot be. p. 233

With respect to the integral relationship between emptiness and nothing within the context of Zen and Taoism, Grigg adds:

> The extension of emptiness is nothingness. . . [Nothingness] is emptiness at its most allowing, if such a definition makes any semantic sense. p. 241

As Lao Tzu, the father of the ancient Chinese philosophy of Taoism, plainly observes in *The Tao te Ching*:

> Become totally empty
> Quiet the restlessness of the mind
> Only then will you witness everything unfolding from emptiness.

Preface

The Vietnamese Buddhist teacher, Thich Nhat Hanh, writing in *The Heart of Understanding*, attempts to allay Westerners' anxiety over the notion of emptiness:

> "Emptiness" means empty of a separate self. It is full of everything, full of life. The word emptiness should not scare us. It is a wonderful word. To be empty does not mean nonexistent. . . .
>
> Emptiness is the ground of everything. Thanks to emptiness, everything is possible. That is a declaration made by Nargajuna, the Buddhist philosopher of the second century. Emptiness is quite an optimistic word. pp. 16-17

Sounding a similar note, the Zen Buddhist scholar, D. T. Suzuki, commented decades earlier:

> Emptiness which is conceptually liable to be mistaken for sheer nothingness is in fact the reservoir of infinite possibilities.

Emptiness has implications with respect to the self as it is understood from a Buddhist perspective. Regarding the self, Zen teacher, Danin Katagiri, points out in *You Have to Say Something*:

Nothing is Empty: A Whole Haiku World

> The absence of our own being is the face of Emptiness. Emptiness is not produced nor is it stopped; it does not appear nor does it disappear. In experiencing the absence of our being, we become fully alive, for we are not dependent on things. This is to be free from suffering. p. 76

The American Beat novelist, Jack Kerouac, echoes Katigiri's view of no-self or egolessness in *The Scripture of the Golden Eternity*:

> Strictly speaking, there is no me, because all is emptiness. . . .
> All is bliss. p. 25

The Taoist sage, Chuang Tzu, pointed out that we humans too often find ourselves angry due to misattributing malevolent motives to others when, in actuality, there is *no one there*. He created a parable about this which Thich Nhat Hanh recounts in *Being Peace* without formally acknowledging Chuang Tzu as the author of the vignette:

> A man was rowing his boat upstream on a very misty morning. Suddenly, he saw another boat coming downstream, not trying to avoid him. It was coming straight at him. He shouted, "Be careful! Be careful!" but the boat came right into him, and his boat was

almost sunk. The man became very angry, and began to shout at the other person, to give him a piece of his mind. But when he looked closely, he saw that there was no one in the other boat. It turned out that the boat just got loose and went downstream. All his anger vanished, and he laughed and he laughed. pp. 33-34

To realize that *emptiness predominates* constitutes a major breakthrough in terms of liberation. In a similar vein, Zen teacher, Shunryu Suzuki, points with a poetic sensibility to the connection between emptiness and enlightenment, though one need not be a Zen meditator or Buddhist devotee to realize enlightenment. As Suzuki Roshi (honored teacher) maintains:

> Although we have no actual written communications from the world of emptiness, we have some hints or suggestions about what is going on in that world, and that is, you might say, enlightenment. When you see plum blossoms or hear the sound of a small stone hitting bamboo, that is a letter from the world of emptiness.

Is it any wonder, then, why Suzuki Roshi implored meditators to honor their beginner's mind, as he does in the passage below? His words of wisdom

Nothing is Empty: A Whole Haiku World

from *Zen Mind, Beginner's Mind* apply no less to aspiring haiku poets:

> If your mind is empty, it is always ready for anything. It is open to everything. In the beginner's mind there are many possibilities; in the expert's mind there are few. p. 21

Let me be clear: I am not trying to tether haiku to Zen Buddhism and Taoism here, which highlight nothingness and emptiness in their teachings. That is not what this haiku book is about. Nonetheless, I do believe that Buddhism and Taoism offer many constructive and provocative insights into the nature of nothingness and emptiness that we might do well to ponder. (1) An early interest in Zen, in fact, stimulated my fascination with nothingness or void and prompted the following poem, which I wrote a number of years ago:

Zen garden
nothing
stands out (2)

To better understand the significance of nothing, perhaps it would be useful to consider an example: *the air we breathe*. It is both commonplace and extraordinary. We cannot see the air we breathe and thus might equate it with nothing, but this same no-thing is vital to our very survival. As such, air is

Preface

something, *not* nothing; even young children are taught to identify the molecules it is composed of. Air is personal insofar as *my* existence is dependent upon this invisible "substance," but it is also impersonal because every other life form likewise depends upon it. Too, we should not forget that air is *empty*; that is, if there is a vase with nothing in it, air easily and effortlessly occupies the space inside. Hence, it is not quite accurate to say that the vase is empty: the vessel contains something we cannot see. (3)

At this point, it should be evident that ordinary language does not adequately convey the depth and breadth of nothing and emptiness. This is why a poetic perspective might be useful, as Eastern philosopher, Alan Watts, writing in *Play to Live*, proposes:

> A poet is always trying to describe what cannot be said. He [or she] gets close, he gives the illusion that he has made it. This is a great art, *to say what cannot be said*. p. 42; emphasis added

For the sensitive poet, who has emptied his or her mind to study the ineffable, there is a quality of grief or poignancy associated with the challenges of expressing the inexpressible. This is what Zen and haiku scholar, R. B. Blyth, articulates in *Games Zen*

Nothing is Empty: A Whole Haiku World

Masters Play:

> To know that there is nothing to know, and to grieve that it is so difficult to communicate this "nothing to know" to others—this is the life of Zen [and poetry], this is the deepest thing in the world. p. 95

Nothing for Bashō

Although contemporary English-language haiku commentators have endeavored to separate haiku from Zen and Buddhism, it is clear that Bashō, the father of haiku, studied Zen off and on over the years, as Makoto Ueda points out in his biography of Bashō. (4) What is less well-known is the significant influence that Taoism appears to have had on the 17th century Japanese poet and itinerant. According to Peipei Qiu in *Bashō and the Dao*, Chuang Tzu's writings, in particular, impressed upon Bashō the importance of emptiness as a foundation for the haiku spirit. To quote Qiu at length:

> The concepts of *kyo* and *jitsu* were first brought into Japanese literary theory by Kukai in the ninth century to imply fabrication versus verisimilitude and falsehood versus truth. The Danrin School [of Buddhism] used the paired concepts to mean "falsehood" and "truth" in

their interpretations of Zhuangzi's *gugen*. The Danrins' usage of the terms to a certain extent influenced Bashō, and his early poetic remarks also took *kyo* and *jitsu* as rhetorical devices, although he emphasized that both *kyo* and *jitsu* must achieve the effect to convey truth. Along with the formation of his notion to "follow *zoka* and return to *zoka*," Basho came to use *kyo* to denote the emptiness of mind as the essential condition of artistic perception and expression, and *jitsu* as the substance of the object treated. Although Bashō does not mention clearly what relationship is between "emptiness" and the "primal breath" and why they can lead to supreme poetic expression, his statements have rich references in the *Zhuangzi*, and a comparative reading of his *haikai* remarks and the Daoist text yields helpful insights into his poetics. p. 144

On the Same Wavelength

Naturally, I am far from alone in endeavoring to express the inexpressible, as the poem below by haiku poet, Bob Lucky (5), will attest. It is not hard to hear the Taoist and Buddhist echoes here:

nothing in the window is everything

Nothing has similarly caught Wanda D. Cook's (6) poetic eye:

> autumn gust
> in the zen garden
> nothing stirs

Consider this, too, by Cook (7):

> haiku moment
> but words fail
> the importance of nothingness

Karina M. Young (8) appreciates how nothing obtrudes:

> nothing
> in the way
> the spring sea

Jungian psychiatrist and haiku poet, David H. Rosen (9)—who doubles as a stand-up comedian—penned this poem suffused with humor that is relevant to the theme:

> Dr. Nada is my name—
> my card
> nothing on it

Preface

Ron C. Moss (10) wrote this beautiful poem on emptiness:

>   moonlit snow
>   the sound of emptiness
>   in the world

Scott Mason has devoted quite a bit of attention to emptiness and nothing. The first relates to the relationship between emptiness and duplicity, while the other two center around nothing. All three poems appear in Mason's book, *The Wonder Code (11)*:

>   empty shell
>   the wind intones
>   my sins of omission

>   ground fog
>   I am certain
>   of nothing

>   nothing
>   remains to be pruned
>   zen garden

In her imitable way, the late Marian Olson (12, 13) apprehended the significance of emptiness and nothing, as evidenced in these two poems from *Sketches of Mexico*:

Nothing is Empty: A Whole Haiku World

> wave after wave
>   takes back
>   the empty shell

> breakfast at the inn
> hot chocolate and a *bolillo*
> nothing special

Allen Ginsberg, dying of cancer in 1997, wrote the following Buddhist-informed death poem, which appears in Patricia Donegan's (14) book, *Haiku Mind*:

> To see Void vast infinite
> look out the window
> into the blue sky

vincent tripi (15), writing in *to what none of us knows*, points not only to the mind of a meditator but to the haiku mind as well:

> Empty mind . . .
>   also i blow
>   on the dandelion

On the nature of nothingness, tripi (16) shares this astute poetic observation:

> nothing to hide water lily closes

Preface

As with the foregoing poets, I too am on the lookout in these pages for emptiness and nothingness to see what truth might be revealed to my otherwise inattentive, conditioned mind. What I discern are the many ways in which nothing and emptiness manifest in daily life.

A Word about Nihilism

Buddhism has often been misunderstood as nihilistic because of the attention it gives to impermanence or transience, which is symbolized by nothingness and emptiness. Nothing could be further from the truth. (No pun intended.) On this question, mindfulness meditation teacher, Sharon Salzberg (17), observes:

> From the Buddhist point of view, it is true that emptiness is a characteristic of all life – if we look carefully at any experience we will find transparency, insubstantiality, with no solid, unchanging core to our experience. *But that does not mean that nothing matters*. emphasis added

Whether or not Buddhism—and Eastern philosophy in general—is nihilistic is beyond the scope of this book. However, I maintain that focusing on the omnipresence of nothing and emptiness in our world is in no way nihilistic. Acknowledging that life is fundamentally empty need not lead inexorably to cynicism, pessimism, numbness or despair. Life is not meaningless by virtue of turning one's attention to nothingness or emptiness. On the contrary, I found this very haiku project to be uplifting, stimulating, intriguing, enlivening. My sense of life has deepened by virtue of studying emptiness through the lens of haiku.

A Cautionary Tale or Two

While an understanding of the true nature of emptiness can deepen one's relation to life-and-death, its misappropriation by the ego can lead to arrogance or self-inflation. Such, I believe, is the message contained in the following old Jewish tale:

> There's an old joke about a rabbi who prostrates himself in the synagogue during the High Holy Days, crying, "Oh, Lord, before you I am nothing!" The cantor likewise prostrates himself and cries, "Oh, Lord, before you I am nothing!" The janitor, watching from the back of the synagogue, gets caught up in the fervor of the moment and joins in. "Oh, Lord," he cries, "before you I am nothing!" The rabbi, taking note of this, nudges the cantor and whispers, "Look who thinks he's nothing." (18)

Can you spot the pomposity, the ego's pretensions

to be pious? Such is the susceptibility in all of us regardless of status, station or attainment.

The Tibetan Buddhist teacher, Chögyam Trungpa, coined the term, *spiritual materialism*, to identify the susceptibility of the ego to self-inflation in the name of spiritual advancement. But the reality is spiritual attainment is not an act of will; it cannot be directly pursued by the ego. That is the paradox: seek and it shall elude you.

Along these lines, there is another anecdote worth telling. It is recounted in a compilation by Paul Reps, *Zen Flesh, Zen Bones*. A university professor comes to a monastery to study Zen and is greeted by the master, Nan-in. He pours the visitor tea until the cup starts to overflow. The professor exclaims that the cup is already full, which prompts the Zen teacher to respond:

> "Like this cup," Nan-in said, "you are full of your own opinions and speculations. How can I show you Zen unless you first empty your cup?" p. 5

What is the point, then, of seeking spiritual realization or understanding? Herein lies the open secret: There is no point. True spiritual realization starts and ends with *emptiness*. There is *nothing* to gain. What we are looking for is already right here and always has been. Haiku attests to this holy truth, which is why I continue to be so enriched by it.

Double Meaning

At the center of *nothing is empty* is a double meaning. Fifty years ago, my friends and I would have found this double meaning to be "trippy." I am going to resist the temptation to elaborate on how *nothing is empty* could embody opposite meanings. This is the mystery within the mystery that is Life. Mystery is what poetry is made of. It is what I leave the reader to ponder because contemplation of mystery can lead not only to insight but revelation, which poetic truth and wisdom depend on.

> long winter night—
> alone on the open road
> *all or nothing*

Notes

1. For the interested reader, there are references on Buddhism and Taoism in the Recommended Reading that I have included.

2. *Flower of Another Country: 2007 HSA Members' Anthology*. W. D. Cook and L. Porter, eds.

Preface

3. Of course, nothing has yet another meaning, which I do not dwell on in this book, but I want to acknowledge, nonetheless: In Hitler's reign of terror during World War II, the Nazis did their best to reduce the Jews and others to nothing—physically, psychologically, spiritually—in horrific concentration camps. The Nazis succeeded in many cases to strip these human beings of everything—including their very selfhood—but not all.

A good many managed, miraculously, to hold onto their humanity, including my aunt and great aunt, Clara Knopfler and Pepi Deutsch, through heroic acts of perseverance. I am in awe of them and others like them, including existential psychiatrist, Viktor Frankl, who developed his own form of therapy based on what he lived through and witnessed in the camps. Their eloquent voices are an eternal source of inspiration to me. See C. Knopfler, *I Am Still Here: My Mother's Voice* and V. Frankl, *Man's Search for Meaning*.

4. M. Uedo. Matsuo Bashō: The Master Haiku Poet. Tokyo: Kodansha International, 1970.

5. *Modern Haiku*, 43.1, 2013.

6. *Modern Haiku*, 41.1, 2010.

7. *bottle rockets*, #17, 2007.

8. *Acorn*, #41, 2018.

9. J. Baranski, and D. H. Rosen, *White Rose, Red Rose*. Eugene, OR: Resources Publications, 2017.

10. *Acorn*, #36, 2016.

11. S. Mason, *The Wonder Code: Discover the Way of Haiku and See the World with New Eyes*. Chappaqua, NY: Girasole Press, 2017.

12. Marian Olson, *Sketches of Mexico*. Northfield, MA: Lily Pool Press, 2012; p. 47. A *bolillo* is a flavorful baguette made in Mexico.

13. Ibid., p. 75.

14. Quoted in P. Donegan, *Haiku Mind: 108 Poems to Cultivate Awareness & Open Your Heart*. Boston: MA: Shambhala, 2010. Also in: R. Epstein, ed. *Dreams Wander On: Contemporary Poems of Death Awareness*. Baltimore, MD: Modern English Tanka Press, 2011. For more death haiku poetry touching on the theme of emptiness or nothingness, the reader is also referred to Yoel Hoffmann's edited collection, *Japanese Death Poems.*

15. v. tripi, *to what none of us knows*. Greenfield, MA: tribe press, 2012; p. 21.

16. ibid., p. 81.

17. Quote accessed online at:
https://www.brainyquote.com/quotes/sharon_salzberg_527433

18. Accessed at Eric Rennie's website:
http://www.godwardweb.org/lookwhothinkshe'.html

Robert Epstein
El Cerrito, CA
5 October 2018

Poems

Nothing is Nothing

Nothing is Nothing

in my highchair
finishing the cake
Mom cries: *all gone!*

Nothing is Empty: A Whole Haiku World

nothing disappoints bare branches

Nothing is Nothing

the toddler's first peek under the bed

all the way down the old well

Nothing is Nothing

where the monarch was a moment ago

where he buried
the gold his grandpa gave him
a big hole

Nothing is Nothing

after cleaning out my desk drawers

looking for change
under the sofa cushions
what she finds instead

walking the void meditation

what the flashlight does when the battery's dead

Nothing is Nothing

the alligator lizard
under the couch
eating nothing

Nothing is Empty: A Whole Haiku World

in the attic w/o my glasses

Nothing is Nothing

up in the middle of the night

Nothing is Empty: A Whole Haiku World

black*out*

Nothing is Nothing

abandoned web
even the prey
vanished

Nothing is Empty: A Whole Haiku World

moving in
she opens the refrigerator
for the first time

Nothing is Nothing

throwing out
the spent daisies
what this vase holds

Nothing is Empty: A Whole Haiku World

questioned
she tells customs
I've nothing to declare

Nothing is Something

Nothing is Something

nothing can get close to it mountain lion

writing
her first surreal novel
nothing makes sense

in her heart
what's left of her love
after years of neglect

back to school
behind the first year teacher
the blank blackboard

Nothing is Something

cutting class
his score
on today's quiz

into the trash
the boy's mother throws
the broken clock

Nothing is Something

covert operatives
ransacking the apartment
for nothing

Nothing is Empty: A Whole Haiku World

gravesite
the widow's eyes
vacant

from her beloved
no communication
nothing

Nothing is Empty: A Whole Haiku World

caught in the cookie jar
my answer when Mom asks
what I'm looking for

Nothing is Something

empty nest
the new puppy
has no clue

quiet sunset
she promises she has
nothing up her sleeve

Nothing is Something

Gulf War vet
still living on
next to nothing

got milk?
the smart aleck says
I got nothin'

Nothing is Something

nothing
between the Crucifix
and the parishioner

Nothing is Empty: A Whole Haiku World

lined up
on the window sills
all their empties

Nothing is Something

---

in the dryer
the missing sock
still missing

in the mom & pop shop after the looting

Nothing is Something

crinkled night
the couple on their porch
nothing between them

Nothing is Empty: A Whole Haiku World

not what I thought under the rock

first blind date
does nothing matter to you?
oh, definitely

Nothing is Empty: A Whole Haiku World

don't ignore
the absence
of bees

Nothing is Personal

Nothing is Personal

what can I say
about nothing; pointing
to my bald pate

nothing to lose
I wade into the river
wearing my b-day suit

Nothing is Personal

midnight foraging
the last piece of pie
missing!

car crash
amnesia's just another word
for nothing

Nothing is Personal

to tell the truth
how much she learned
in college

it's not true
he's doing nothing
tv

Nothing is Personal

she emerges
from her deep sea dive
empty-handed

what could it mean . . .
no fortune
in the cookie

Nothing is Personal

in her room
dancing to the pop song
I'm nothin' without you

Nothing is Empty: A Whole Haiku World

---

how often
Mom said, it's better
than nothing

Nothing is Personal

late stage cancer
what the oncologist
gently recommends

Nothing is Empty: A Whole Haiku World

retired with nothing to do

Nothing is Personal

---

empty fitting room
nothing
shows itself

into the shower wearing *you-know-what*

what's that on the tip of my tongue

Nothing is Empty: A Whole Haiku World

what you read between the lines

Nothing is Personal

open grave
before lowering the casket
into the ground

Spring Lake
oars up
drifting

Nothing is Impersonal

Nothing is Impersonal

returning the next day
for what had been
her walking stick. . .

Nothing is Empty: A Whole Haiku World

the canvas before the brush tip touches it

Nothing is Impersonal

live mouse trap
except for the nibbled cheese
nothing

Nothing is Empty: A Whole Haiku World

on the sidewalk
a blue egg hatches
nothing

Nothing is Impersonal

what remains
after the seagull cracks open
the clam shell

open bird cage open window

Nothing is Impersonal

to whom does it belong
nothing
in the lost & found

Nothing is Empty: A Whole Haiku World

there a minute ago
the beagle looks everywhere
for the ball

Nothing is Impersonal

what's left when the table's cleared

in the meantime
what we hear, waiting
for the wind again

Nothing is Impersonal

why does it matter
that fleeting moment after
emptying the trash

after the last snow melts nothing

Nothing is Impersonal

just the flagpole

first, senior moments
later, dementia
full immersion in. . .

Nothing is Impersonal

    the public fountain
      suddenly stops
      the afterflow

nothing (in the sky) is unbreakable

Nothing is Impersonal

believe me
she says
it's nothing

Nothing is Empty: A Whole Haiku World

nothing in the eye of the storm

Nothing is Impersonal

before it was a tide pool

Zen garden
nothing
stands out

Nothing is Impersonal

nothing fades away

… Emptiness is All

Emptiness is All

emptiness interrupted the spittoon

Nothing is Empty: A Whole Haiku World

before turning it
half the hourglass
empty

Emptiness is All

---

what the space
surrounding the bell
covers

randomly picking
a pistachio from the bag
empty

Emptiness is All

---

poof!
the magician opens
his empty palm

Nothing is Empty: A Whole Haiku World

what
the gorge
reminds
her of

high up the trail except for her shadow. . .

Nothing is Empty: A Whole Haiku World

agate beach
a little girl looks for nothing
in particular

is silence something or nothing?

the sound of a concert hall emptying

Emptiness is All

after his last breath *what?*

staring into space the possibilities

spotting *it* at the farthest point on the horizon

Nothing is Empty: A Whole Haiku World

what's what *beyond the stars*

unasking
your Original Face
before your parents were born
what we really know

that bud right smack in the middle of the mystery

nothing could be a revelation

Recommended Reading

Blyth, R. H. *Games Zen Masters Play: Writings of R. H. Blyth*. R. Sohl and A. Carr, eds. New York, NY: New American Library, 1976.

Chuang Tzu, *Basic Writings*. B. Watson, tr. New York, NY: Columbia University Press, 1964.

Grigg, R. *The Tao of Zen.* Rutland, VT: Charles E. Tuttle Co., 1994.

Hanh, T. N. *The Heart of Understanding: Commentaries on the Prajnaparamita* Heart Sutra. P. Levitt, ed. Berkeley, CA: Parallax Press, 1988.

_____. *No Death, No Fear: Comforting Wisdom for Life*. New York, NY: Riverhead Books, 2002.

Hoffman, Y., ed. *Japanese Death Poems*. Rutland, VT: Charles E. Tuttle Co., 1986.

Katagiri, D. *You Have to Say Something: Manifesting Zen Insight*. S. Hagen, ed. Boston, MA: Shambhala, 1998.

Kerouac, J. *The Scripture of the Golden Eternity*. San Francisco, CA: City Lights, 1960.

Recommended Reading

Kornfield, J. *A Path with Heart: A Guide through the Perils and Promises of Spiritual Life.* New York, NY: Bantam, 1993.

Krishnamurti, J. *Freedom from the Known. San Francisco, CA: HarperSan Francisco, 1969.*

Lao Tzu, *The Tao Teh Ching.* S. Mitchell, tr. New York, NY: HarperCollins, 1988.

Loy, D. *Lack and Transcendence: The Problem of Death and Life in Psychotherapy, Existentialism, and Buddhism.* Amherst, NY: Humanity Books, 2000.

Mitchell, S., comp. *The Second Book of the Tao.* New York, NY: Penguin Press, 2009.

Nishitani, K. *Religion and Nothingness.* J. V. Bragt, tr. Berkeley, CA: University of California Press, 1962.

Qiu, P. *Bashō and the Dao: The Zhuangzi and the Transformation of Haikai.* Honolulu, HI: University of Hawaii Press, 2005.

Reps, P., with Senzaki, N., comp. *Zen Flesh, Zen Bones: A Collection of Zen and Pre-Zen Writings.* Garden City, NY: Doubleday & Co.,1957.

Rumi, J. *The Essential Rumi.* C. Barks with J. Moyne, tr. San Francisco, CA: HarperSanFrancisco, 1995.

Recommended Reading

Sartre, J-P. *Being and Nothingness: An Essay on Phenomenological Ontology*. H. E. Barnes, tr. New York, NY: Washington Square Press, 1984.

Sayama, M. Samadhi: *Self-Development in Zen, Swordmanship, and Psychotherapy*. Albany, NY: State University of New York Press, 1986.

Sengstan. *Hsin Hisin Ming: Verses on the Faith Mind*. R. B. Clarke, tr. Virginia Beach, VA: Universal Publications, n/d.

Suzuki, S. *Zen Mind, Beginner's Mind: Informal Talks on Zen Meditation and Practice*. New York, NY: Weatherhill, 1972.

tripi, v. *to what none of us knows*. Greenfield, MA: tribe press, 2012.

Ueda, M. *Matsuo Bashō: The Master Haiku Poet*. New York, NY: Kodansha, 1982.

Watts, A. *Play to Live. Selected Seminars by Alan W. Watts*. South Bend, IN: and books, 1982.

www.ingramcontent.com/pod-product-compliance
Lightning Source LLC
Chambersburg PA
CBHW071120090426
42736CB00012B/1964